Tabl

Skill 10

Skill 11

Skill 12

Skill 13

Skill 14

Skill 15

Skill 10, Passage 1

The Falcon's Splendid Plan

The day looked dark and dismal as the sun rose over the grasslands. The rain just would not stop as the sun, which had been absent, tried to peek through the clouds and warm the earth. Mother Falcon went in search of food while her young falcon was hidden in the brush. The mother bird thought that the thicket would be a safe place for the young falcon to wait.

In the grassland the adult lion woke. While stretching his tired legs, he roared as he felt his hunger. He wanted something to eat. He caught sight of an object in the distant thicket and began to watch just in case it might serve as lunch. With a sudden start, the young falcon popped his head up thinking his absent mother should be back soon. He too wanted something to eat and was waiting for his mother to bring tidbits of fresh food to the nest.

The lion knew the young falcon would make a splendid snack. Mother Falcon was not far away. She flew over and watched the lion. She was frantic about this dismal problem. Her instinct told her of the lion's plan, and she was committed to making sure her young bird was safe.

Mother Falcon flew like a rocket to disrupt the lion's plan. At that instant the lion began to charge after the mother falcon but tripped over a fallen tree stump. The lion's leg caught under the stump, and he could not extract it. The lion was frantic and knew he would die if he couldn't adjust his leg to free it from the stump.

Continued >>

Mother Falcon flew close to inspect the problem. Because she was not mean, she couldn't leave the lion to die in the grassland. She flew over the lion and asked, "If I help extract your leg, will you consent to keep us safe in our home in the thicket?"

The lion didn't want to be a victim of the fallen log and swore he would spend his life guarding the falcon family. Mother Falcon told the lion of her splendid plan to extract his leg. "The problem is really very easy to solve," laughed the falcon. "First, stop thrashing. Then dig a large hole with your free paw, and your leg will slide right out."

The lion was impressed by the falcon's splendid plan. Now the new friends will spend hours basking in the tall grasses, and Mother Falcon and her young falcon will always be safe and content.

Title and Passage: 424 words

Swimming with the Dolphins

Today is just like any other day for Annell and Mallin. They happen to live near a calm, tranquil beach on Hampton Road. They leave their house before dawn while it is still dark and walk to the beach to watch the sun come up over the Atlantic shore. The twins spread their blanket on the cool sand and hear the splash of the current as it pushes waves on the shore.

"This is the best time of day. The sun looks like a splendid ball of fire as it floats in the sky. It looks like droplets of water are falling off the sun and back into the ocean," cried Annell. "The sea is so clear and bright after the sun first comes up."

"Let's swim and look for shellfish in the tranquil, blue sea," suggests Mallin. "Mom said it would be fine if we stay close to the beach." The twins begin to run, but they are watchful as they step into the wet sand. They start splashing each other and dipping their heads under the waves. Annell isn't watching to see how far she has gotten away from the shore. All of a sudden she has a problem. She isn't as strong of a swimmer as her twin brother Mallin and is very scared.

She tries to swim to shore, but the current is too strong for her. She starts thrashing about as the waves engulf her. All of a sudden she spots what looks like a hundred dolphins swimming near her. The school of dolphins are jumping in the tranquil sea. One of the biggest dolphins pauses from the games and begins to watch her. It makes shrill sounds

Continued >>

like a signal as it swims up next to her and begins flapping its fin. "Oh no!" screams Annell. "I think it wants to hurt me."

"I think it wants to help you," yells Mallin. "Grab its fin."

Annell is bashful as she reaches for the gray fin. "I think you are right; it wants to save me," she yells back. "This is a very smart mammal." She holds on tight to the wet fin as the dolphin begins pulling her close to the shore. A second dolphin swims up on the other side of her. She holds on to both dolphins as they swim. All of a sudden the dolphins shake loose and jump straight up. Annell stands on the sand on the bottom of the sea. She looks back to thank her new friends as they swim back into the sea.

Title and Passage: 430 words

The Bathtub Race

The town of Sumphill is getting set for the Bathtub Race. Each summer the town hosts a race where teams push carts made of bathtubs. This year Linnet and Brandon Jackson can join the contest because they are the right age.

Weeks before, Mom and Dad start to search for an old bathtub for their children to use for the race. Mrs. Jackson talks to Mrs. Rambrum, who lives in the house on the northwest side of the street. Mrs. Rambrum says that she'll give them the old bathtub that is sitting on the side of her house. The children are so thankful, and they begin work on their bathtub.

The siblings choose a classic plan that would be easy to make. Mr. Jackson adds a steering wheel to guide the bathtub. Brandon concocts two sets of tires and connects them to a rod so the bathtub can roll. Linnet finds some ties to connect the steering wheel to the rig. When it is done Mr. Jackson inspects the cart to make sure there will not be any mishaps. Mr. and Mrs. Jackson, Linnet, and Brandon use a spectrum of colors to paint their bathtub.

On the day of the big race, the Jacksons push their bathtub to the starting line. The ringing bells tell them it is time to start. They are off and running! Brandon pushes the bathtub, and Linnet sits in the tub and steers. Down the lane they go. Brandon is cutting in and out of the other bathtubs. They are now in third place. Brandon yells at Linnet, "There is excess weight in the bathtub. Can you

Continued >>

throw anything out?" Linnet looks around for things to throw over the side. First, she throws her jacket out, but that only helps a little. Next, she throws out her sun glasses, but that doesn't help at all. Then she takes off her tennis shoes and throws those over the side. That does it! Faster and faster the two siblings fly. Brandon is whipping over the lanes. Like a rocket he flies down the path passing the other bathtubs.

Linnet leans forward as far as she can, sticking her hand out in front of her. She breaks through the ribbon at the end of the race just one second before the others. Brandon and Linnet are shocked because they are the youngest contestants to ever win the Sumphill Bathtub Race.

Title and Passage: 405 words

Skill 11, Passage 1

Snakes

Snakes are reptiles. This means they are cold-blooded and need to keep their bodies warm or cool by the sun, shade, and water. Snakes can be found in both warm and cool places. They can be seen in places such as grasslands, hidden in the cracks of limestone, and even in lakes. Snakes have been found in high altitudes on hillsides and at sea level. They are almost everywhere except for places like Iceland. They are rarely found inside.

Reptiles also have scales on their bodies. It is said that there are over 2,900 kinds of snakes. Snakes come in all sizes and colors. Some have bodies encased in striped scales, others are spotted, and still others have extremely bright prints on their scales.

Snakes don't have legs. They must move by sliding through the landscape. Their undersides have rough scales. This helps them grip branches and slide across limestone and rocks.

People who study wildlife have said that reptiles that have striped scales and live in warm places are more likely to escape an enemy, crawl away, and not attack. Some snakes with spotted scales that live in colder places are more likely to engage the enemy and attack.

Snakes, like other reptiles, eat meat. They search the landscape for small fish, birds, and other animals. This would include other reptiles and small mammals. Huge snakes have been known to eat a small pig or even a deer or

Continued >>

antelope. When they eat, their jaw disengages and makes them look misshapen. Their teeth are backwards so that their food cannot escape. The snake will excrete venom to stop the food from moving.

Many snakes feed on small mammals, reptiles, and insects that could be harmful to man. This helps to keep the number of these pests down. Not all snakes have venom that will harm us. We must learn to recognize when a snake is unsafe but concede that snakes can be helpful to us, too.

Title and Passage: 330 Words

My Huge Mistake

Excitement filled the air at band practice. My school's band was chosen out of hundreds of bands to play at our state's big ballgame at halftime. Fifty-five high school students would get to fly to Dallas, Texas, on a jetliner and march onto the field.

We started to have more practice time. The drumline compiled five songs that would both inspire and impress the crowd. My best friend, Tredmane, played his trombone like he had never played before. Shinlane ramped up her skill on the bagpipes, and I worked so hard on my bass drum that my hands were sore.

All fifty-five students, eight teachers, three moms, and even one dog piled into the school bus for the short trip to the landing field. All of our instruments were safely encased in hard plastic cases to keep them safe for the flight.

Tredmane and I stayed in a room together, and we invited Jackson and Zane Fishbine to stay with us. We had a lot of fun jumping on the beds and chasing each other around the room until our band teachers came to check on us. We got to stay bunkmates as long as we took their advice and confined our antics to some other place.

The big day arrived at last. We were ready to invade the field and give the show of a lifetime. First, the trumpets, trombones, flutes, and other wind instruments marched onto the field in exact step with one another. The other units joined, and our drumline was at the end.

Continued >>

It was going so well! Each person played their part perfectly. The entire band stepped exactly where they were supposed to. Then it happened—the worst mistake I could ever have made. Everyone else marched left, but I mistakenly sidestepped right. I collided with the trombones, and we all fell onto the field in a great big pileup. My head got stuck inside Tredmane's trombone, and my feet were entwined in Shinlane's bagpipes. It took several of the game's athletes to pick me up and take me to the sideline to free me from the mess. I was feeling badly that I had been ungraceful and made an extreme problem for the band.

When we got back to our bus I was very contrite, but my bandmates were not at all blameful. I am glad I have such extremely kind friends. But next time, I think I will be more careful to watch which way my bandmates are going. I don't want to make any more huge mistakes.

Title and Passage: 427 words

The Whalebone Find

School was over, and summer had arrived. The students and teachers had been confined in classrooms all year and were glad for summer break. Excitement was everywhere. There would be swimming, camping, and baseball games. Justin Fladgate was going to be 10 years old. His dad told him he could invite five friends to Wickmane Beach to celebrate with a camping trip. They would find a campsite, build a campfire, set up tents, and spend the night.

Justin was frustrated that they had to wait for two weeks for the party. The day arrived, and it was time to load the truck. Before reaching the beach, they drove through the city admiring the landscape. The group chose a nice dockside spot to set up camp. Mr. Fladgate built a raging fire in the rock fire pit. The boys helped set up the tents before they sat around the campfire and engaged in telling chilling stories. Bedtime was extremely late, and the tired boys went inside their tents to sleep. They dreamed of great new quests for the next day.

The next morning the sun rose in the sky, exposing water that cascaded over jagged rocks. The boys wanted to walk on the beach. Mr. Fladgate told them they could go just to the edge of the rocks. He would stay at the campsite and make pancakes and eggs for breakfast.

The boys inhaled the fresh air as they began hiking toward the cascading water. Justin tripped over a twiglike object. He stopped to inspect it and found that it was

Continued >>

entwined in yellow kelp that had washed up on the rocks. Justin recalled the last time he had gone for a swim here. Kelp had been twirled around some sticks that had washed up on the beach then, too. The boys worked very hard to free the twiglike object from the flat, leafy vines and brought it back to the campsite.

After Mr. Fladgate completed his inspection of the twiglike object, he told the boys that it was a very exciting find. The complex object was a whalebone. He said that some whales do not have teeth, but instead they have a stemlike plate on each side of their upper jaw. This helps them to sift out unwanted objects as they are eating. The boys were excited about the whalebone and were going to take it home to show their other friends. They concluded that this was the best campsite ever and made plans to come back every summer.

Passage: 423 Words

Life in the Congo Basin

The Congo Basin is located in Central Africa. More than 400 species of mammals, 1,000 species of birds, and 700 species of fish can be found there. This vibrant place could rival any zoo on the planet!

The hot and humid climate of the basin makes it an excellent home for many kinds of plants and animals. One of these is the female rock python snake. For her, the heat is vital to the care of her large brood of eggs. This lethal reptile is a superb mom. She suns to warm herself and then returns to the nest to wrap herself around her eggs to keep them warm. She must do this until her eggs hatch, which takes about 90 days.

Grown rock pythons grow to be 30 feet long. You might think this lady python would dine on rodents and other small living things. Beware! You might regret getting too close to this jumbo snake. Rock pythons have been known to swallow antelopes, pigs, goats, and even crocodiles!

The Congo Basin is most well-known for the number of primates that make their homes in the more remote spots. One of these is the bonobo. Bonobos are closely related to chimps but are smaller and darker. Much is unknown about bonobos. Because of the remote nature of where they live, it is hard to study them. Bonobos and another Congo native, the sun-tailed monkey, can only be found in this location, which is a haven for primates.

Continued >>

Two other species also found nowhere else are okapis and bongos. The okapi is somewhat like a horse with stripes that help it blend into the dense Congo forests. Bongo antelopes have long, curved horns and bright stripes on their bodies. Since they like to live in dense remote places, few bongo antelopes were seen by man until the 1960s.

Humans have lived in the Congo Basin for many years. The basin provides food, fresh water, and homes to more than 75 million people. The humans living in the rain forest are smaller than the humans of the grasslands, which makes them move about the forest more easily than taller humans. They live in tribal groups of 15 to 70. They live as nomads, moving to new parts of the forest as needed, carrying all they own on their backs. When they decide to live in a spot for a while, they cut and clean away only as much brush as needed and they remain under the thick cover of the trees. This means that after they leave a spot, nature can quickly reclaim the space. These forest nomads trade their goods with others who live in the village but always return to the forest. It has been shown that these nomadic tribes have better diets and health than others in this part of Africa.

Title and Passage: 478 words

No Time for Regret

Toby took a deep breath and inhaled the fragrant air. He had to remind himself that this was no dream. All of this was real. Stepping out of the cab at the airport, he did a quick check to make sure he had all of his items. The sun was blazing as he tried to locate his photo ID for the trip. Found it! Now he could begin this new phase of his life. The driver gunned the motor, reminding Toby that he needed to focus. He was taking too long to respond to the driver's request to have the fare paid. With his wallet open, he took care of that small item.

He turned to take one last look at his home. Toby was an Ohio native, and he knew he would return. He spotted a distant silo and thought of his dad's farm near Avon Lake. He could smell the lilacs and knew he would miss those cozy moments of sitting on the porch of his mom's tidy little condo when everything began to bloom in the spring. He smiled a secret smile, knowing it would all wait for him. This was no time for regrets!

As he made his way through the lines to catch his plane, he took a moment to relive the last few weeks. He wanted to savor every last event. Looking at the label on his bag reminded him of his school days. While not a great student, his final grades were good enough to attend a small, private college not far from home. His desire was to take biology classes and get a job with a wildlife group. He began to take photos of the animals he studied. His work was noticed by

Continued >>

a global news agency, and now he was on his way to China. His duty was to take photos for a local TV channel that was doing a story on the Siberian ibex and the need to protect this species. Even now, Toby could not believe his luck.

Toby would start his trip on a jumbo jet. Once he got to China, they would move everything to a private biplane. After a night in a hotel, he would join the film crew for the final leg. He hoped his trusty tripod and other tools would not be lost. He had been careful to label each item. He knew he would not relax until he and his tools were united again.

Once on the plane, he found a vacant seat and tried to pretend he was not scared. He was silent as others got into their seats. Soon a kind lady sat beside him, chatting as the plane began to taxi for takeoff. As the music of the engines got louder and louder, Toby couldn't resist one last look at the place he called home.

Title and Passage: 479 words

A Win for David

Nathan finished the last of his bacon and sopped up the last bit of gravy on his plate. It was time to leave the hotel and go to the show! On this sultry July day, he would see his sibling fly a biplane and be an acrobat at the same time. David was his hero, and that's all there was to it.

David had been a navy pilot and was now flying with stunt pilots from Idaho Falls. Now that David was retired, he could devote his time to what he loved best. For Nathan, this was a chance to get close to pilots and planes. He was the baby of the family, but he did not regret that. Not for even a moment! He had come to rely on David and loved to be with him. Nathan was sure that David was about to provide him plenty of fun. He had even made a small wager with his dad. He was betting that David would win the top place trophy. He couldn't resist hoping for luck as David hopped up on the wing of his biplane to get cozy in the cockpit. His copilot was in his seat and produced a thumbs up signal for David. The siren blared two blasts and they were off.

The biplane rapidly climbed and began to rotate. As the crowd watched it spiral, they cheered and clapped. There was a moment when the biplane's wing dipped so close to a cement wall that viewers held their breaths. The next thing they all knew, David and his copilot were buzzing a vacant structure as they sped across the field to spin upside down near a silo. Dust rose like a cyclone. The crowd cheered with

Continued >>

gusto as David retraced the flight path for round two. As the meter ran down on the time for this event, David did one more crazy spiral, and just as the final siren went off, he landed the plane crisply and safely.

David and his copilot deplaned and made their way to the stage to wait for their score. The judges took their time with the total. When they added the points for each spiral, they decided David would get a bonus that would give him the trophy! Nathan and his family began to laugh and cry all at once. What a moment this was!

Nathan was silent as he watched the trophy being placed in David's hands. He took time to reflect on the amazing man David had become. In his private dreams, he wished he too could have devoted his life to duty in the navy.

In the blazing July heat, David spoke, reminding all that this moment could only happen because of his time in the navy. David wanted to ask people to donate so he could begin a new program where retired navy pilots can focus on educating students about life in the navy and the job of pilots. His hope was that his stunt flying would help to promote this dream. Nathan had a lot of respect for his brother and his new crusade.

Title and Passage: 524 words

The Life of a Lighthouse Keeper

Have you ever daydreamed of what it might be like to care for the beacon that keeps ships safe? There was a time when lighthouse keepers protected ships, making sure their voyages were safe and helping to avoid shipwrecks.

Each lighthouse had its own blinking pattern to help seamen clearly know where they were at nighttime. In daylight it was even easier to tell since each lighthouse was built to appear like no other nearby lighthouse. The ship captains and lighthouse keepers used flags to send messages. When a ship needed help, flags were hoisted shipboard to relay messages to the lighthouse. The lighthouses used their flags to relay news about wind and weather.

One key job of the keeper was maintaining the lenses of the lighthouse beacon. Soft linen cloths were used for cleaning the beacon lenses. Cloths were drawn across the windows to protect the beacon from daylight.

Lighthouse beacons were turned off during the daytime to save fuel costs, which was the biggest expense of a lighthouse. If the lighthouse was to run cheaply, the light could be turned on in the daytime only if something happened, such as a shipwreck. Then, a lamp could remain lighted past daybreak.

The process of getting ready to light the beacon began well before dusk. First the keeper inspected the lenses, which were newly cleaned that morning. Next, the lamp that produced the light was checked and the fuel was

Continued >>

refilled. The wick was then trimmed and lighted. The keeper would remain for at least half an hour after lighting the beacon and would visit the light at least twice between dark and daylight.

Sadly, the job of lighthouse keeper has mostly disappeared in the United States. However, if this is what you've been dreaming of doing, don't despair. There are programs that will allow you to maintain your dream and become an employee of the lighthouse even if it's only briefly. You must send a request to the owners of the lighthouse to see if you have the skills they are seeking. If they agree that you would make a good lighthouse keeper, then you could be appointed to that role for a weekend or more.

For these volunteer lighthouse employees, the daily chores begin just after daybreak. The volunteer lighthouse keeper tunes the radio to hear the day's weather and then begins by raising the weather flags. The owners may provide a list of jobs to maintain the upkeep of the lighthouse. When the daily task list is completed, the volunteer employee may indeed enjoy some of the benefits of life on the seacoast. Some volunteers enjoy walking the beach looking for seaglass. Heading out in a sailboat allows for a pleasant afternoon. One of the best benefits of the role of volunteer lighthouse helper is hearing the sound of waves beneath the lighthouse at nighttime. There is nothing better than the peaceful sleep that follows a busy day at a lighthouse.

Title and Passage: 500 words

Steelhead Lake

It is week one of the Mountjoy family's summer season at Steelhead Lake. Colleen stares dreamily at the beachfront as the pontoon boat filled with rowdy teens passes by. In a way, she wishes she could be out there carousing with them, but she knows she will never be allowed. Her mom and dad don't allow her to ride when there is a boatload of kids ever since her eighteen-year-old brother had narrowly escaped drowning last year when a speedboat filled with too many gleeful teens capsized. Colleen would always recall her relief when she learned that her brother and her friends were safely pulled out of the water.

She really doesn't mind the rules. Speedboats kind of scare her, anyway. She is content to float around in her dad's old rowboat, which has been very carefully maintained over the years. Because of his constant care and upkeep, Colleen has a rowboat that is a keepsake for her and is admired by all.

Colleen recalls when she was eight and her dad painted the rowboat to look like a rainbow. When Colleen saw it, she was delighted at how cheerful it looked. Her parents like it because it makes her easy to spot on the lake from the windows of their beachfront home.

Each weeknight while they are at the lake, Colleen takes her little rainbow rowboat out before the daylight is gone. Colleen really enjoys rowing to the rearmost part of the lake where there is a tiny lagoon filled with

Continued >>

duckweed. Duckweed are aquatic plants found floating on the top or just beneath the water, and they look like a green bedspread spreading across the lagoon. The plants somehow have been carried into the lagoon by the overflow and remain there until a rainy spell. Colleen loves to watch for the bullfrogs and bluegills who fed on the duckweed. Each evening she comes home faithfully before the sunlight fades, pleasing her parents. Just thinking about this nightly jaunt brightens Colleen's day!

Just then, Colleen bolts upright and recalls what today is. Today she starts sailing school! All of the Mountjoy children spend weekdays during the season at Steelhead Sailing School. This is Colleen's first year. She quickly gathers her things and heads away from the beachfront to get to the sailing school at Bounder's Dock in time for her class. She has been reading about the parts of a sailboat for her entrance exam. Mainsail, topsail, gooseneck, and mainmast—she knows the meaning and use for all of these and more. She has been faithful to her dad's wishes and has spent the last fifteen days with her nose in the sailing handbook. She cannot wait to announce that she has easily passed her test! This time next lake season, daytime will be spent sailing and evening rowboating. Life will be good at Steelhead Lake!

Title and Passage: 479 words

Storm at the Campground

It was the end of a wonderful week of camping. Aiden, Grayson, and Sandeep were the last of the scouting troop to leave the clubhouse. Mr. Fielding, their leader, was outside in the driveway, loading heavy boxes into the van. The three boys had been outside playing football when Mr. Fielding announced they were heading home after completing one last task.

The boys had complained loudly when they heard they had to clear the heavy containers out of the storeroom. They believed they needed to be outside, enjoying the campground one last time before leaving this place. Instead, here they were, underneath the kitchen counter, breathing heavily from their hard work. The rest of the scouting troop had been allowed to escape without scrounging around in dirty storerooms. How unfair!

Just then they heard a loud crack of thunder followed by howling wind and a screeching sound. Mr. Fielding came bounding into the room shouting for the boys to move away from the windows. They could hear the sound of something bouncing off the car. It was hailing! They heard a screeching sound, which they realized was a snapped limb of a beech tree scraping on the tin roof. As the boys were looking out the window, they saw the breaking limb come pounding to the ground right at the same spot where Mr. Fielding had stood. They were all relieved that the scouting leader had made it inside safely. Mr. Fielding had come in just in time.

Continued >>

As the howling and screeching continued, it began to get dark in the clubhouse. Mr. Fielding told the boys not to be frightened. He explained that they were quite safe in the clubhouse and could even camp there an extra week if they had to. They had plenty of supplies. He said, however, that he had every reason to believe the bad weather would be over soon. He asked Aiden to bring the flashlights in from the bedroom so they would have plenty of light. Suddenly, along came the loudest booming noise yet. This noise was followed by a huge crack and the screeching of metal. Mr. Fielding was groaning as he looked out the window. There was the car, with the right fender crushed under the heavy tree limbs. The boys could not contain their dismay. Mr. Fielding went right to soothing them, explaining that it would all be fine. The car would be taken care of at no cost to him.

Mr. Fielding picked up his phone and called the nearest towing shop. Frowning, he hung up the phone and turned to tell the boys what he had just found out. Instead of heading home tonight, they would be waiting until at least the next afternoon for the tow truck. The camping trip was not over for this threesome! Sunlight came peeking in the windows as the boys began to carry their bedsheets and packs back into the bedroom.

The boys were looking at each other secretly. It was hard to conceal their excitement. To extend this great camping trip was too good to be true. This was going to be fun!

Title and Passage: 526 words

The Riggle and Ziggle Grand Show

My Uncle James made a promise to take me to the festival when it comes to our home town of Trumble, and today is the day. Thousands of people line up to make their way inside the gigantic tent. Uncle James and I make a noble attempt to not stumble over people as we climb the stairs to find our seats. At last we settle in to watch the show.

The lights dim and a very loud, deep voice booms, "Ladies and gentlemen, children of all ages, welcome to the Riggle and Ziggle Grand Show." The crowd noise begins to dwindle as the audience decides to settle in for the show. The spotlight zooms around the tent and stops on the middle ring. Three clowns come in riding unicycles and begin to juggle foam basketballs. The little clown rides the tallest unicycle and keeps tilting like he's going to fall. Suddenly, there's an obstacle and the unicycle begins to wobble. It is easy to see that he is in trouble. The unicycle flies out from under him and he rolls across the floor, knocking over a second unicycle. Both clowns' feet become tangled, and they begin to tumble across the floor. All the people in the crowd giggle. We are having the best time!

Once again the lights zoom in and out, landing at the top of the tent. There is an acrobat on a very thin wire with a bicycle. Her costume is made of jewels that sparkle when the lights hit them. The acrobat begins to ride across the wire on a bicycle. She starts to wobble on the wire, and the

Continued >>

people watching let out an audible gasp. I don't know how it is even possible, but she made it across safely.

Next it is time for the animals to come out. First, a poodle walks out on its hind legs and begins to dribble a little ball. A tiny beagle joins the poodle. The beagle fumbles the ball, which knocks the poodle off its hind legs. A very tall clown runs to the middle ring with a hoop. The beagle and the poodle jump through the hoop while running around the ring. The poodle runs behind a big box and comes out with a teeny, tiny saddle on its back. The beagle jumps into the saddle, and they run around the ring.

The last part of the show is the elephants. Five elephants, each with a saddle on its back, come out and follow one another around the ring. Acrobats with dazzling costumes sit in the saddles. The man with the deep, loud voice yells a command. The elephants raise their front legs and are very gentle as they place the acrobats on their backs. The crowd lets out an audible hooray. The juggling clowns on the unicycles and the poodle with the beagle riding on his back join the elephants on the stage.

The Riggle and Ziggle Grand Show is over. It was the best night of my life! I can't thank Uncle James enough for bringing me.

Title and Passage: 518 words

Life in the Frindle Forest

Deep in Frindle Forest lives a family of beetles. Each day the family shuffles through the tangled trees searching for insects and leaves to nibble on for their meal. The parents keep a watchful eye on their four beetle babies to make sure they don't stumble over any obstacles that might harm them. The beetle babies giggle and play all day in the forest. Soon the littlest beetle uncovers an object that sparkles in the sun, and so he begins to nibble on it. Finding the object to be extremely hard, he grumbles that the object wasn't very soft or tasty. Mother beetle laughs and says, "Son, you can't eat that. It's a pebble."

Later that day as they are shuffling through the trees, the middle beetle stumbles upon some water that bubbles up from the ground. The bubbles tickle his nose each time he tries to crawl to the edge of the water. All four babies play with bubbles and forget all about looking for food. The beetles live a carefree, simple life, and they love the Frindle Forest.

While the family sits next to a pile of pine needles, they notice the sun has dwindled down to only a speck of light. Father Beetle looks at the sky and sees dark black clouds begin to block the sun. He calls to his family, telling them to go safely to the log. The beetles fumble around trying to pick up their belongings and stumble into the log just as a gentle drizzle of rain falls from the sky. The babies are startled and begin to cry when they hear a rumble and a

Continued >>

crackle of lightning fills the sky. Mother and Father Beetle know that trouble is ahead because soon the log will begin to fill with rain. The rain will fill the log, and they won't be able to scramble away to safety.

"Hurry," says Father. "We must paddle to the tree and climb up under the leaves to stay dry." The beetles paddle out of the log and scramble up the maple tree to wait for the rain to stop. But the rain doesn't stop. The beetle family huddles together as the rain continues to come down. The babies tremble as they cling to Mother and Father Beetle.

Finally, the rain begins to dwindle, and the dark black clouds clear. A bright dazzling rainbow spreads across the sky. The beetle family huddles together as they watch the sky sparkle with color. Noble eagles and nimble deer creep from their hiding places to search for food. Frindle Forest is once again alive with animals. The beetle family shuffles down from the maple tree to resume their hunt for food and their simple life in the forest.

Title and Passage: 463 words

Cable Cars

Have you ever ridden in a cable car? There is a long history of cable cars in our country. One of the very first types of cable cars was built in New York City and was called a street car. Long rails were placed in the middle of the cobblestone streets. The street cars were pulled along rails by either a single horse or multiple horses. When people wanted to ride the car, they would stand on the side of a cobblestone street and wave at the person driving. When someone wanted to get off the cable car, he pulled on a strap inside the car. The strap would startle the driver, who would then stop.

The cable car, which is different from a street car, is in use today in San Francisco, California. A man named Smith Hallidie developed the cable car in this city to solve a problem. One day many years ago he saw a horse drawn street car have a horrible accident on a cobblestone street in San Francisco. As Mr. Hallidie watched, horses struggled to pull a heavy load up a steep hill. The horses were in trouble because the load was too heavy and they were unable to pull the street car to the top. It took only a couple of minutes before they tumbled to the bottom, killing all of the horses. This spectacle troubled Mr. Hallidie, and he sought a way to prevent this debacle from happening again.

The San Francisco cable cars use a wire rope or cable that is under the rails that were already located in the middle of the street. The cable, which is attached to the car,

Continued >>

allows the cable cars to move slowly along the rails. Horses are no longer needed. The cable car driver has a handle that lets him move or idle to allow people to get on and off the car. At the end of each rail line there is a table that turns so the cars are capable of a couple of things, like going around angles.

Cable cars almost became extinct because people love driving automobiles. In many cities in the US, cable cars were replaced by gasoline cars and single and double deck buses.

Today one of the only cable car systems still thriving is in San Francisco. People are able to ride the cable car to and from work as well as for sightseeing trips. For example, many who visit the city take the cable car to famous sites like Chinatown. Be careful not to stumble on the stairs when climbing on board. Also, hold on to the special poles that are provided so you won't tumble into other people as the car goes up and down the steep streets. Stay safe, settle back, and enjoy a ride on one of the most famous cable car systems that exists!

Title and Passage: 482 words

Monster Trucks

Marvin loves to attend Monster Truck Rallies with his parents. They watch the colorful gigantic trucks thunder around the track. He is awestruck as the engines roar past him in pursuit of the finish line. Secretly Marvin imagines himself the driver of his very own truck named Thunder Bolt that is decorated with bright yellow lightning bolts.

One day his dad returns home from work with a very ordinary truck. Dad is extremely excited and tells Marvin they are going to turn this truck into their very own Monster truck. Marvin is thrilled and asks if perhaps they might call it Thunder Bolt. Dad agrees and says that is a perfect name. Marvin and his dad make a trip to the hardware store to purchase the tools they need to transform the truck from ordinary to a sparkling performance truck.

The two partners work very hard to install enormous tires so the truck will travel high above the ground. They argue about the color to use but finally determine that it should be sparkling purple with bright yellow lightning bolts on either side. They hunt for a lift so they can raise the body of the truck even farther off the ground to improve performance. Dad is able to barter with a store manager and get a bargain price. When they finish, the truck looks like it has a purple suit of armor and is ready to race.

Dad enters Thunder Bolt in the next Monster Truck Rally. They are so excited to be participating in a real race. It will be held the afternoon of December 3rd. Marvin is

Continued >>

extremely nervous, and he worries that maybe his dad shouldn't be driving the truck. After all, it could be harmful to his dad or the precious truck. He would never forgive himself if something horrible happened. All he could think about is whether he should tell his dad to forget competing and to forfeit the race.

On the day of the race Dad reports to the starting line while Marvin sits with other family members who have come to observe the race. The horn sounds and the race is on. Thunder Bolt starts in last place. Marvin is alarmed when he observes his dad turn a corner and two of the giant tires lift off the ground. He is certain he is about to see a rollover accident. Dad is no coward. He maneuvers the truck expertly around the corner and is now in third place. The finish line is in sight and Dad races as hard as he can. All of the people in the stadium are on their feet cheering for Thunder Bolt to go faster.

Dad crosses the finish line in second place. At first, Marvin is sad that his truck wasn't a winner. He thinks about it and realizes how fortunate he is that his dad not only survived his first race but did better than either of them had expected. Dad and Thunder Bolt really are winners.

Title and Passage: 505 words

Alligators

Alligators are interesting creatures. They are considered reptiles, which means they are cold-blooded and covered in scales. Alligators are part of a larger group called archosaurs. Surprisingly, this is the same group that includes both birds and dinosaurs. Modern-day birds and alligators share the same breathing method, left over from their shared archosaur heritage.

If the smaller gators survive to become adults, they will grow to an average of 8 to 11 feet long. Their bodies make them look as though they are wearing a suit of armor with large eyes bursting through the armor on the top of their head. They have a very long nose that turns upward, and it helps them breathe while their body is still underwater. If you look closely in the water you might see what looks like a floating log. Take care! That log may end up turning out to be a submerged alligator gliding through the shimmering marsh.

Alligators live in many places in the United States. Scientists estimate there are around one million gators in the Florida waters. One of the best places to see a gator is in the National Everglade Park. However, in Florida they can be found anywhere and everywhere there is fresh, slow-moving water. Florida gators have been observed in lakes, marshes, ponds, canals, and once in a while in backyard swimming pools. Visitors need to be alert and careful where they step near water. That bumpy rock may really be an

Continued >>

alligator resting on the bank.

During cooler temperatures alligators move slower and will dig a long burrow-like tunnel that is filled with water and mud to protect them from the cold. Once warmer weather arrives, you will find the alligators stretched out in the sun along the edge of the bank or submerged in the water with only a nose and bulging eyes peeking through.

Even though the adults have no natural enemies, gators were once on the endangered species list. This means there were very few of them left. Hunters would capture them and use their armored skin to create purses, belts, and shoes. Hunting alligators is now monitored so they won't become extinct.

Gators will eat almost anything that moves but don't usually pursue humans unless they get too close. If you see an alligator it is very important that you do not try to move closer to poke or feed it. Keep your distance because they can move faster than a horse, running up to 20 miles per hour in short bursts.

Even though there are a surprisingly high number of alligators in Florida, there have been only 17 people who didn't survive an attack from 1948 to 2005. Most of the people who suffered a gator attack were trying to capture or pick them up. Visitors should be encouraged to travel to Florida and have a wonderful time. Just leave the alligators alone!

Title and Passage: 484 words

Butterflies in the Amazon

The Amazon Rainforest is the largest rainforest in the world. It covers around 1.7 billion acres and is hot and rainy all year long. The broad leaves of many trees create a canopy so dense that the sun can hardly be seen. Rubber trees, Strangler Fig, and Red Cedar trees are just a few of the 16,000 species of trees that provide shelter for a large variety of rare plants and animals.

The rainforest is filled with many living organisms whose survival depends on its ecosystems. Deep in the rainforest there are as many as 150 different species of gorgeous, delicate butterflies. These marvelous creatures are considered to be members of the insect family. It's hard to believe that this graceful and delicate creature has a fine layer of scales covering its wings.

Butterflies begin their lives as eggs that hatch and form larva. During the larval stage the organism is known as a caterpillar. The very hungry caterpillars spend all their time eating flowers and leaves until they are ready to rest in the chrysalis stage. Magic happens inside the chrysalis, and finally the caterpillar is transformed and a beautiful butterfly emerges and spreads its wings.

The rainforest provides a wonderful place for butterflies to thrive. Trees provide a covering for the ground as well as glittering waterfalls. This is perhaps the most perfect place on Earth for them to live. Butterflies can only fly when the temperature is over 86 degrees. Pilots have reported seeing huge groups of butterflies flying above the treetops, fluttering in the sunshine.

Continued >>